Engineering Marvels

Roller Coasters

Dividing Fractions

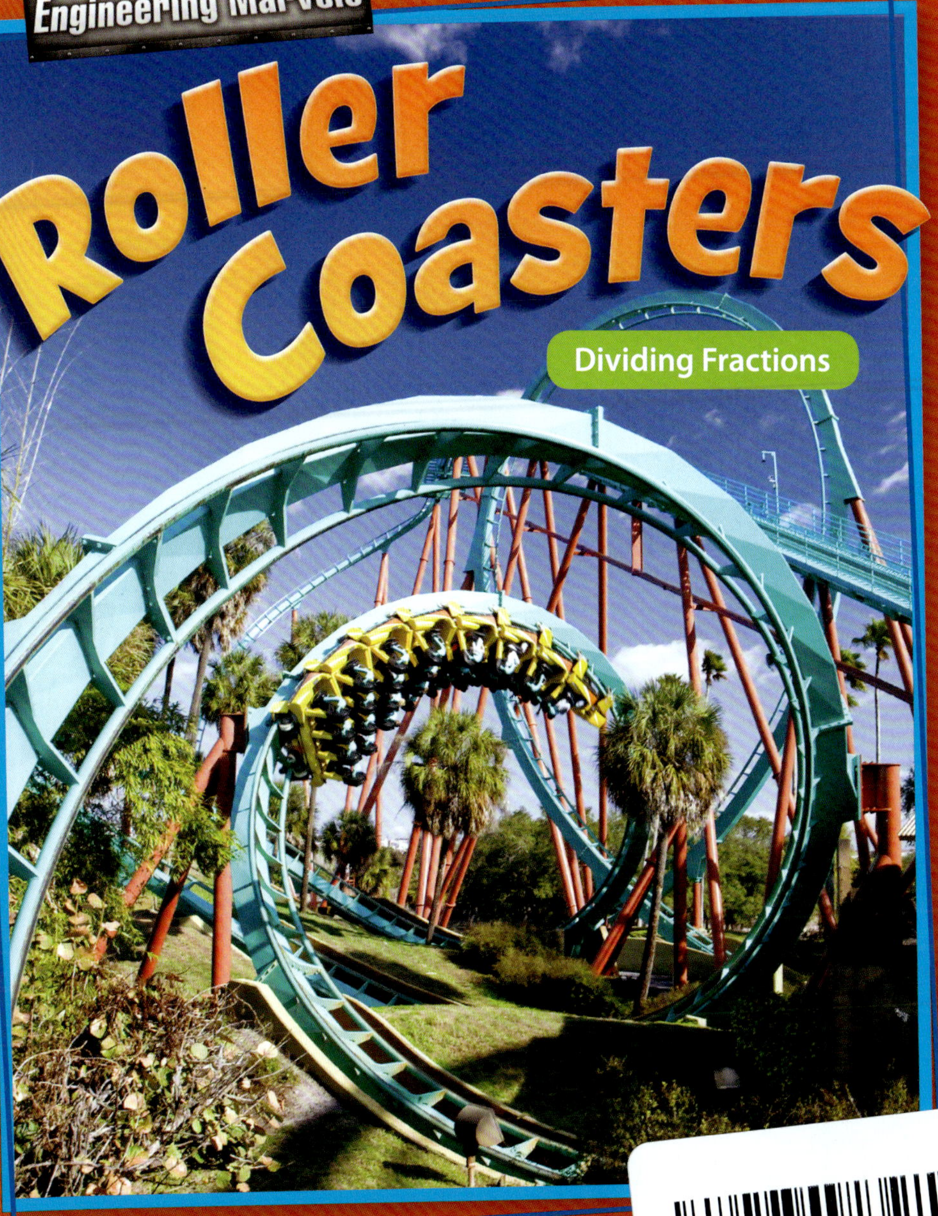

Ben Nussbaum

Consultants

Lisa Ellick, M.A.
Math Specialist
Norfolk Public Schools

Pamela Estrada, M.S.Ed.
Teacher
Westminster School District

Publishing Credits

Rachelle Cracchiolo, M.S.Ed., *Publisher*
Conni Medina, M.A.Ed., *Managing Editor*
Dona Herweck Rice, *Series Developer*
Emily R. Smith, M.A.Ed., *Series Developer*
Diana Kenney, M.A.Ed., NBCT, *Content Director*
Stacy Monsman, M.A., *Editor*
Kristy Stark, M.A.Ed., *Editor*
Kevin Panter, *Graphic Designer*

Image Credits: pp.3–4 George Sheldon/Shutterstock; p.5 (top) Heritage Image Partnership Ltd/Alamy Stock Photo; p.7 (top and bottom) Jeremy Thompson; p.8 Popperfoto/Getty Images; p.9 Andy Cross/The Denver Post via Getty Images; pp.10–11 John Greim/LightRocket via Getty Images; pp.14–15 Ben Schumin; p.16 Eric Raptosh Photography/Getty Images; p.17 Allen. G/Shutterstock; p.18 pointbreak/Shutterstock; p.20 Pack-Shot/Shutterstock; p.21 Ian Dagnall Commercial Collection/Alamy Stock Photo; pp.22–23 David Ball/Alamy Stock Photo; p.24 Duane Marden/rcdb.com; p.29 Arina P. Habich/Shutterstock; p.31 Cassiohabib/Shutterstock; all other images from iStock and/or Shutterstock

Teacher Created Materials
5301 Oceanus Drive
Huntington Beach, CA 92649-1030
http://www.tcmpub.com

ISBN 978-1-4258-5817-9

Printed in China WAI002

Table of Contents

The Big Day

"Wake up, sleepyheads! Don't you remember that today is our birthday? We can't be late." Mom and Dad roll over in bed, blink their eyes, and yawn.

Zachary and Elizabeth are twins. They have been looking forward to this day for a long time. To celebrate their birthday, the family is going to Excitement Zone, an amusement park.

Soon, the twins are eating breakfast while Dad packs for the trip. "We have to be at Excitement Zone when it opens," says Elizabeth, as she eats her scrambled eggs.

"That's when the lines for the roller coasters are shortest," Zachary adds.

"I'm looking forward to it," replies Mom.

"I'm looking forward to coming back home," Dad mutters from the kitchen. He doesn't really like roller coasters. Elizabeth quickly reminds him that he promised to ride at least one roller coaster.

The twins have been reading about coasters to prepare for their special day. On the drive, they tell their parents about Russian Mountains. These man-made sledding hills were popular in parts of Russia hundreds of years ago. "They're sort of like the parents of roller coasters," declares Elizabeth.

early 1800s roller coaster

LET'S EXPLORE MATH

Zachary and Elizabeth pack some snacks for the trip to the amusement park. They have 2 pounds of trail mix. Each container holds $\frac{1}{4}$ of a pound. How many containers can they fill? Use the model to solve the problem and complete the sentence frames to describe it.

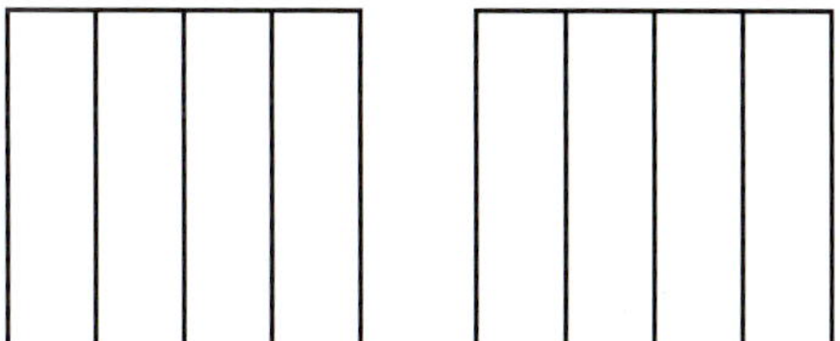

There are ______ groups of ______ in ______.

The El Toro at Six Flags Great Adventure in New Jersey is the biggest wooden roller coaster in the world!

Wooden Coasters

Excitement Zone isn't far from the family's house. Soon, the family is parking. "Perfect timing," says Zachary. "The park opens in a few minutes."

"Look! You can see the top of Wild Wolverine from here," shouts Elizabeth.

"That's the wooden coaster, right?" asks Mom.

"Even I know that," Dad says with a smile before Zachary or Elizabeth can answer.

The twins have been talking about these coasters for weeks, so the whole family feels like experts. Wild Wolverine is the only wooden coaster in the park. For a long time, all roller coasters were made from wood. Most new coasters are now made from steel. Elizabeth is excited as she stares at the tall structure.

The kids found out a lot of facts during their research. Wooden roller coasters have some special **properties**. The wood always changes a little bit. Humidity, or moisture in the air, makes the wood **expand**. On hot days, the wood **contracts**. The change isn't big, but it happens. Because the wood changes, the ride is always a little different. The ride might feel bumpier one day than the next. But, some people prefer the bumpy ride!

"There's a wooden roller coaster in Pennsylvania that was built in 1902. It still runs!" Elizabeth exclaims.

"Our great-great-great-great grandparents could have ridden it," responds Zachary.

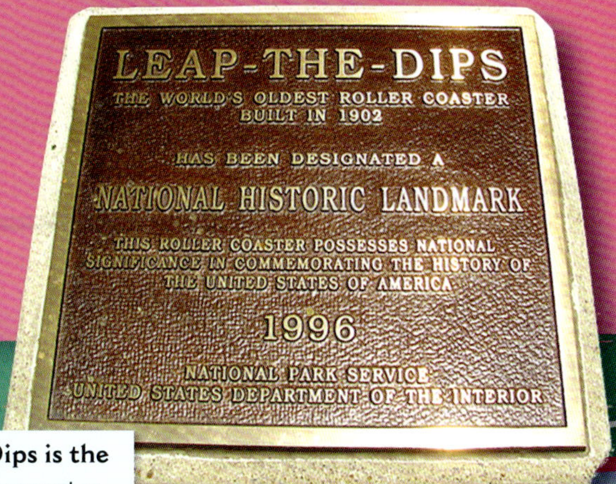

Leap-the-Dips is the oldest roller coaster in the United States.

Safety First!

"All that wood looks extremely **rickety**," Dad says. "If we're the first people riding it today, aren't we kind of testing it? Maybe we should hang back and let other people go first."

"Trust me, it has been tested **thoroughly**," Elizabeth answers.

"But, the park's not even open yet," Dad replies.

"**Maintenance** people get here before the sun rises," Elizabeth explains. "They climb all over the coaster. They're called trackwalkers."

Workers perform maintenance on a roller coaster in England in 1958.

Crash test dummies test a roller coaster in New Jersey.

"After they inspect everything," Zachary adds, "they test the coaster. They use sandbags to **simulate** the weight of riders."

"I suppose that makes me feel a little better," says Dad.

"They also check other things, such as emergency brakes," Zachary chimes in. "The whole process takes hours. And when the park is closed for the winter, all of the cars are taken off the tracks. They are taken apart, cleaned, and parts are replaced if needed."

"I think working on a roller coaster would be really fun," says Elizabeth. "As long as you're not terrified of heights."

"You have to be strong, too," says Zachary. "Trackwalkers take a lot of equipment with them as they climb the ride!"

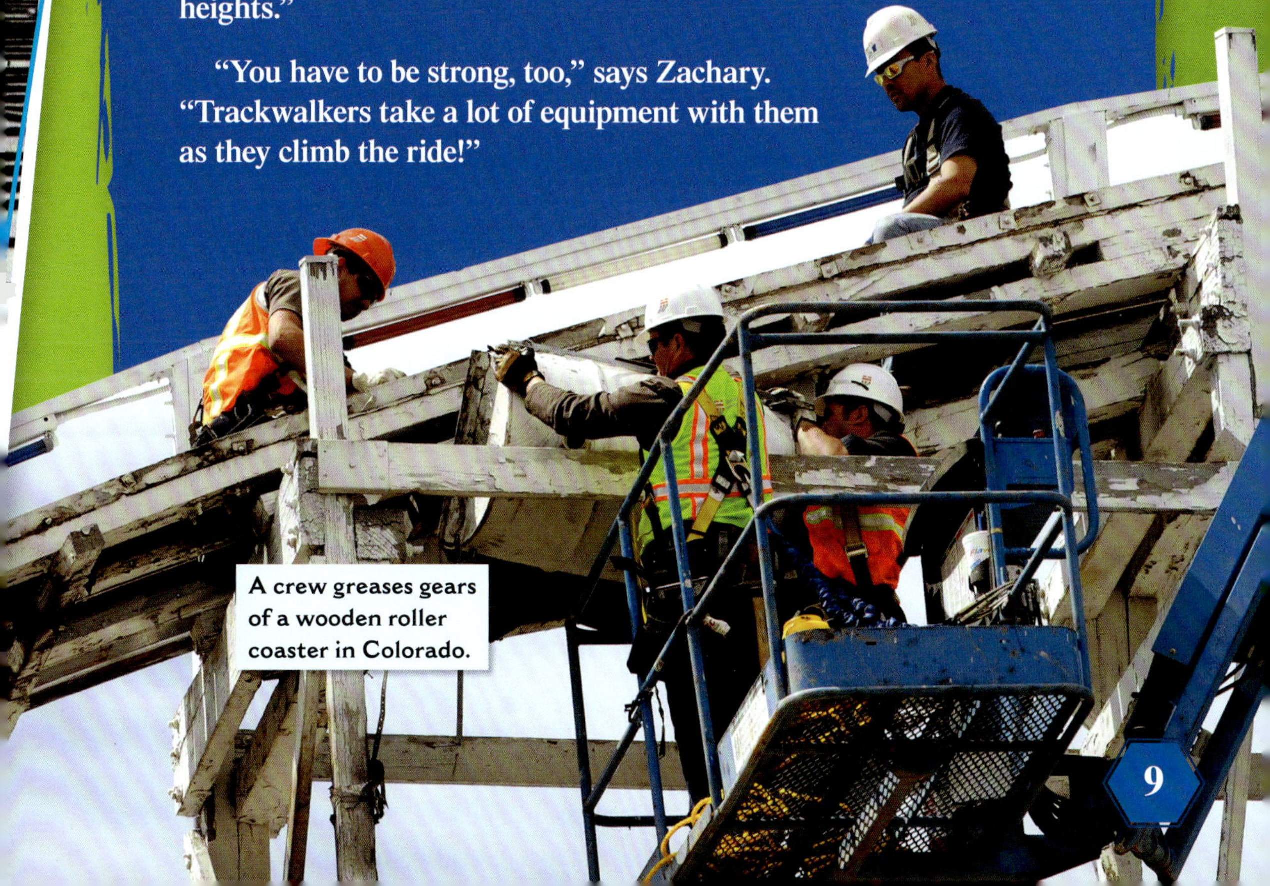

A crew greases gears of a wooden roller coaster in Colorado.

Ready to Ride

The amusement park's gates swing open. Zachary and Elizabeth make a direct path to Wild Wolverine, ignoring all the bright, loud rides along the way. Nothing's going to distract Zachary and Elizabeth today.

"We're the first ones here!" shouts Zachary when they arrive at the wooden roller coaster.

The family walks through a gate and up some steps to Wild Wolverine's loading platform. They sit at the very front of the ride.

"We'll go as soon as the train is full," Elizabeth says.

Mom looks at her with a confused expression. She hasn't ever heard it called a train.

"What we're sitting in is called a car, and the cars of the coaster link together to make a train," Elizabeth says.

"That was a very thorough explanation," Mom teases.

When all the seats are full, the ride's operator checks each car, making sure doors are shut and lap bars are locked in place. The train gently moves forward and slowly starts up a steep hill.

"By the way, Dad, did you know this ride has a **head chopper**?" asks Zachary.

"What!?" Dad starts to say, but his voice is cut off as the coaster plummets down the first hill into a dark tunnel. The coaster shoots back up into the air. It rockets up and down small hills.

The cars connect to form a train.

LET'S EXPLORE MATH

Excitement Zone has a Kiddie Zone with rides for very young guests. Kiddie Zone is $\frac{1}{3}$ acre. It has 4 rides that each occupy the same amount of land. How much of an acre does each ride occupy? Use the model to solve the problem and complete the sentence frames to describe it.

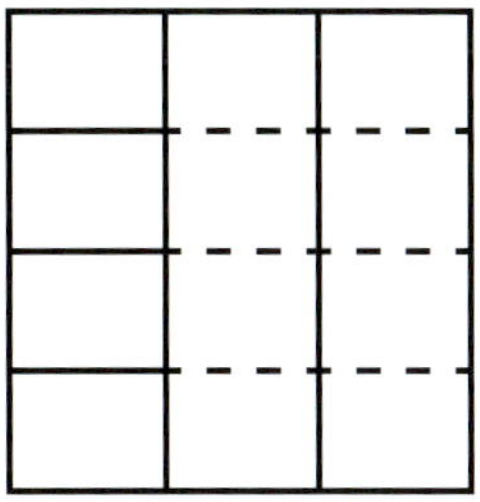

When $\frac{1}{3}$ acre is divided into _______ groups, there is _______ acre in each group.

Head Choppers and Lift Hills

After a couple minutes of pure **adrenaline**, the train slowly rolls back to the loading platform. Zachary and Elizabeth excitedly jump out. Dad looks a little nauseated, and Mom helps him climb out of the car.

"Well, that was my one roller coaster for the day," Dad says. "And by the way, what in the world is a head chopper?"

"A head chopper is kind of a roller coaster illusion. It's when you think that you'll hit your head on something," Zachary explains. "Remember when the coaster went into the tunnel?"

"Of course I remember!" Dad declares. "That was terrifying. I ducked my head!"

"That's a classic head chopper. But don't worry, they are totally safe!" Elizabeth exclaims. "They just seem scary because the train is **accelerating**, turning, and twisting. People can't accurately judge the amount of space above their heads."

"Well," Dad says, "my favorite part was going up the big hill at the beginning. That part was very calm and pleasant!"

"That's called the **lift hill**," says Elizabeth. "The train is pulled up the lift hill by a chain. Then, gravity takes over for the rest of the ride. This is true for the majority of roller coasters."

A train is pulled up a lift hill.

Hypercoasters

After Wild Wolverine, the twins lead their parents to the park's newest roller coaster, Awesome Antelope.

"This coaster is incredible," proclaims Zachary. "It's the only hypercoaster in the entire state."

"A hypercoaster is at least 200 feet (61 meters) tall or has at least a 200 ft. (61 m) drop," says Mom proudly. "You taught me that yesterday, remember? The first hypercoaster opened in 1989, at an amusement park in Sandusky, Ohio."

While they wait in line, the family watches the ride. The train seems to take forever to reach the top of the enormous lift hill.

hypercoaster

It then plummets almost straight down before it makes a few turns and goes up and down hills as passengers scream with delight.

"Look at that **airtime**!" Elizabeth shouts.

"I remember what that means, too," says Mom. "It's when you seem weightless when the train **crests** a hill. Your bottom literally lifts right out of the seat."

"It's physics," says Zachary. "Your body has **momentum** going forward. When the train drops rapidly, your body keeps moving straight forward. You come right off the seat!"

"All of that sounds amazing, but I'll be right here on the ground taking pictures," Dad says with a smile.

A train hurtles over a lift hill on Intimidator at Carowinds in North Carolina.

LET'S EXPLORE MATH

Dad takes pictures while everyone else rides the coaster. He wants to calculate how many pictures he can take before his camera runs out of memory. The camera has 5 megabytes of memory. Each picture is $\frac{1}{4}$ of a megabyte. How many pictures can he take? Use the number line to solve the problem and complete the sentence frame to describe it.

0 1 2 3 4 5

There are ______ groups of ______ in ______.

It's time for Zachary, Elizabeth, and Mom to ride the coaster. They climb onto the loading platform and step into the car.

"Where are the straps?" Mom asks with a confused look on her face.

"There's only a lap bar, like on Wild Wolverine," Elizabeth says.

"I thought for sure we would be secured with straps or a **harness** on a hypercoaster," Mom nervously replies.

"A ride that is supposed to give maximum airtime and doesn't go upside down, normally doesn't have straps," asserts Zachary. "Straps would stop you from feeling like you're floating!"

The ride operator checks that riders are secure. Mom inspects the lap bar.

"Is it supposed to jiggle a tiny bit?" she asks Zachary and Elizabeth.

The twins reassure her, but she isn't convinced. She raises her hand and the operator returns.

"It's exactly how it should be," he tells her after he examines it. "But, you should always ask if you don't feel safe!"

Seconds later, the train starts to climb the lift hill. Then, it charges downhill. It picks up incredible speed, and it races up and down many smaller hills.

lap bar

Powered Coasters and More

When the family is back on solid ground, the twins decide that they need a break from big coasters.

"Let's see what else is at the park," says Mom. "I want to explore for a little bit."

The family rides a swinging pirate ship. They spin around in teacups. They crash into each other in bumper cars. Then, they go on more rides that twirl, drop, and fly.

"There's no line over there," says Elizabeth, pointing to a ride called Power Possum. "It's a kiddie coaster."

"Technically, it's a powered roller coaster," says Zachary.

"According to some people, a powered roller coaster isn't really a roller coaster," adds Elizabeth. Their father looks confused.

"Well, a roller coaster *coasts*," explains Elizabeth. "Once it drops down a lift hill, it runs on gravity. But, a powered roller coaster runs on electricity the entire time. It runs at a constant speed, too."

There's no line, so the family climbs in—even Dad. Dad likes the ride because it does not have huge drops or fast speeds. "That is the perfect type of coaster for me," declares Dad.

LET'S EXPLORE MATH

Powered roller coasters can travel around short tracks several times. How many times does each train travel around its track? Write equations to solve the problems.

1. The ride is 3 minutes long. Each loop around the track is $\frac{1}{3}$ of a minute.
2. The ride is 3 minutes long. Each loop around the track is $\frac{1}{2}$ of a minute.
3. The ride is 1 minute long. Each loop around the track is $\frac{1}{4}$ of a minute.

After lunch, the family goes on an old-fashioned Ferris wheel. It's Mom's favorite ride.

"I know exactly what I want to do next," says Zachary. "Let's go over there," he says, pointing toward a fenced-off area.

"There's nothing in that direction," Dad declares.

"Not yet, but something will be there soon," Zachary insists. "They're building a new coaster."

As the family gets closer, they can see that construction has already started. There's a large rectangular hole in the ground.

"That hole is going to be filled with water. It's where the **splashdown** is going to be," Elizabeth states.

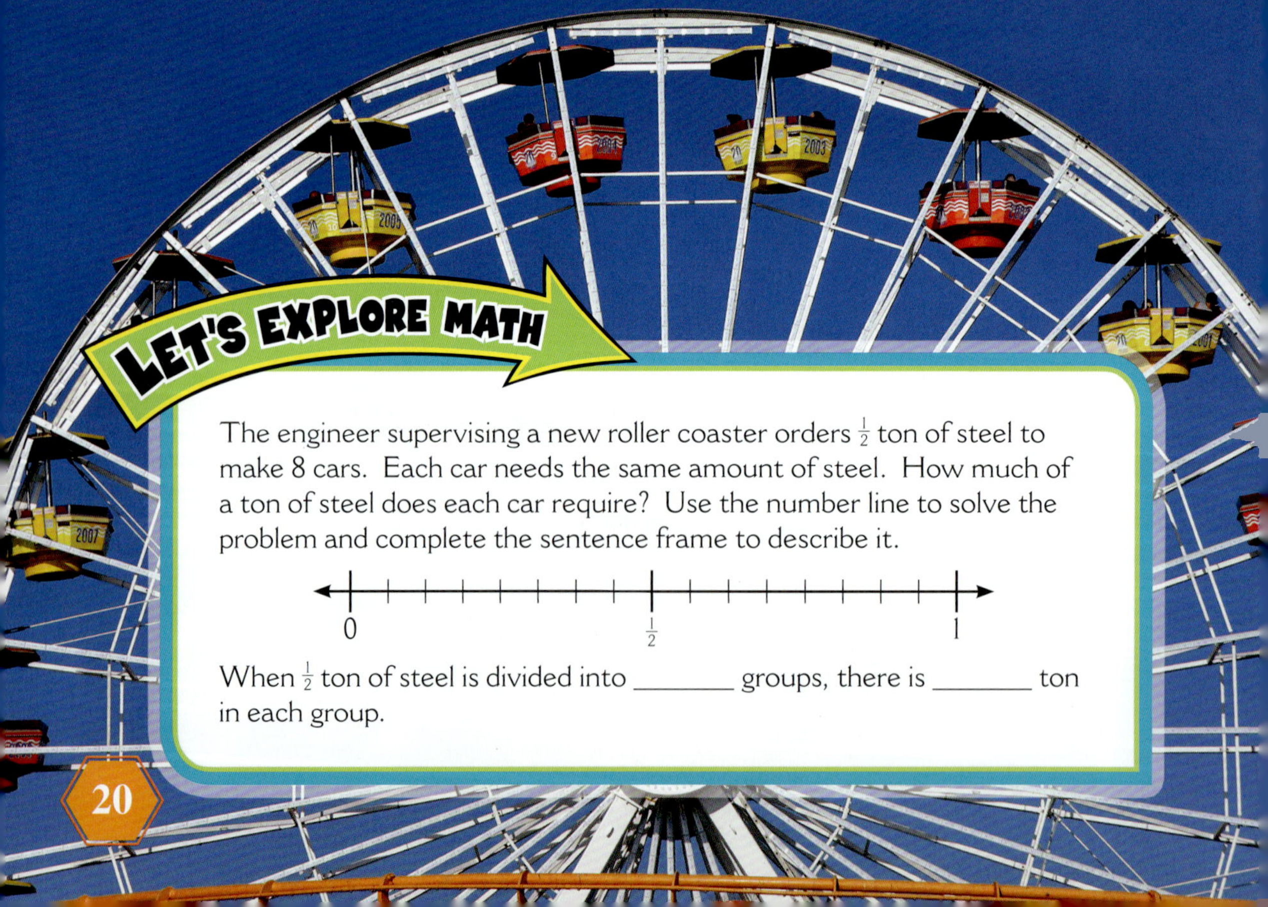

LET'S EXPLORE MATH

The engineer supervising a new roller coaster orders $\frac{1}{2}$ ton of steel to make 8 cars. Each car needs the same amount of steel. How much of a ton of steel does each car require? Use the number line to solve the problem and complete the sentence frame to describe it.

0 $\frac{1}{2}$ 1

When $\frac{1}{2}$ ton of steel is divided into _______ groups, there is _______ ton in each group.

The twins explain that this roller coaster will be called Perplexed Penguin. Toward the end of the ride, the train will appear to splash into the water.

"This splashdown is another type of illusion," Zachary says. "None of the passengers actually get wet."

He explains that two tubes stick out from the back of the train. The rest of the train stays dry, but the tubes briefly dip into water. They're specially shaped to create a huge funnel of water that soars behind the coaster.

"When we come for our birthday next year, Perplexed Penguin will be open," says Elizabeth.

Riders enjoy a splashdown at the end of a roller coaster in Florida.

Roller Coaster Inversions

"We saved the best for last," Elizabeth says. The family walks toward Iguana, the park's most popular roller coaster.

"There are five **inversions** on this coaster!" Zachary exclaims. "We go upside down five times!"

"Tell me about the types of inversions on this ride," Dad says.

"First, we do a **vertical** loop, which is probably the most basic kind of inversion," says Elizabeth. "The train goes up and around in a big circle. At the top of the circle, the train is upside down."

"It's not a real circle, it's more like a teardrop shape," adds Zachary.

"Then, we go into an Immelmann loop, which is like a vertical loop but with a twist at the top," says Elizabeth. "It's named after a **maneuver** that airplane pilots used in World War I."

"Two corkscrews come next. The track rotates 360 degrees to form a corkscrew shape," says Elizabeth.

"Then, the ride moves into a **heartline roll**, or barrel roll. It is when the ride twists 360 degrees around a central point—your heart! The train often dives down as it twists," says Zachary.

As the family waits in line, they watch Iguana. They listen to its passengers scream as it twists around the track.

LET'S EXPLORE MATH

The popcorn at Excitement Zone's snack bar comes in several sizes. Imagine that visitors want to share the popcorn equally. How much popcorn will each person get? Write equations to solve the problems.

1. A $\frac{1}{2}$ pound bag of popcorn is equally shared by 4 people.
2. A $\frac{1}{3}$ pound bag of popcorn is equally shared by 3 people.
3. A $\frac{1}{4}$ pound bag of popcorn is equally shared by 2 people.

"Five inversions seems like a lot," says Mom. "Is that some kind of record?"

"There's a roller coaster in China with 10 inversions," Zachary replies. "And there's one in England that has 14 inversions. It's called the Smiler."

"A more appropriate name would be the Screamer!" Dad jokes.

After they watch the train go around the track a few more times, the family reaches the front of the line.

"I've got an idea," Mom says anxiously. "I can keep Dad company on the ground! I don't need to experience an inversion."

Zachary and Elizabeth wave to their parents as they walk up to the loading platform. The ride operator securely straps them in with a belt and a shoulder harness. There's no way they can fall out of this ride.

Riders twist through an inversion on Chimelong Paradise in China.

The train climbs to the top of the lift hill, but it suddenly stops halfway. Zachary and Elizabeth look around in confusion. They see the ride operator climbing the steps next to the lift hill.

When he reaches the train, he tells a passenger that cameras aren't allowed. With an embarrassed expression, the man hands over his camera.

A Happy Birthday

After the delay, the train climbs the rest of the lift hill and charges downhill. It speeds through each of the inversions, starting with the vertical loop and ending with the heartline roll. When Zachary and Elizabeth are unstrapped, they run over to their mom and dad.

"That was incredible!" screams Zachary with an enormous smile on his face.

"Can we ride it again, please?" begs Elizabeth.

"We only have a few more hours left at the park," Mom responds. "What else do you want to do?"

"Let's ride each roller coaster one more time," Zachary says, as Elizabeth smiles and nods her head in agreement.

The family hustles back through the park, and the twins ride each roller coaster again. As the sun starts to set, the family happily munches on pizza and cotton candy. All around, the park is a blur of activity. Park lights sparkle against the purple sky, and excitement fills the air.

"This is an amazing birthday," Elizabeth says. "Thank you, Mom and Dad!"

"This is the best birthday present ever," Zachary agrees.

"Should we come back here next year?" asks Mom.

"Yes!" the twins say together.

Crowds enjoy roller coasters and other rides at a park in Germany.

Problem Solving

As soon as the twins get home, they start making plans for their next visit to Excitement Zone.

1. If Zachary and Elizabeth spend 2 hours at each roller coaster, how many times can they ride each one? (Time includes ride and wait time.)
    a. Wild Wolverine: $\frac{1}{5}$ of an hour.
    b. Awesome Antelope: $\frac{1}{3}$ of an hour.
    c. Iguana: $\frac{1}{6}$ of an hour.
    d. Perplexed Penguin: $\frac{1}{2}$ of an hour.
2. If Zachary and Elizabeth equally share the snacks, how much of each snack will each twin get?
    a. $\frac{1}{2}$ pizza
    b. $\frac{1}{3}$ pound of French fries
    c. $\frac{1}{4}$ quart of frozen yogurt

Glossary

accelerating—changing speed over time

adrenaline—a substance the body releases in times of stress, excitement, anger, or fear

airtime—the feeling roller coaster riders experience as they rise out of their seats due to the change in speed

contracts—becomes smaller

crests—reaches the highest point

expand—to become larger

harness—a set of straps that connects things

head chopper—a roller coaster illusion in which riders think they will hit their heads on something

heartline roll—a barrell roll movement that twists riders 360 degrees around a central point

inversions—upside down positions

lift hill—part of a track where a roller coaster is pulled up

maintenance—taking care of things through repairs or replacements

maneuver—a skillful procedure or action

momentum—the speed of an object in motion

properties—special qualities or characteristics things possess

rickety—not well made

simulate—to look, feel, or act like something else

splashdown—a roller coaster visual effect where the ride interacts with water

thoroughly—completely

vertical—standing up and down

Index

Answer Key

Let's Explore Math

page 5:

8 containers; 8; $\frac{1}{4}$; 2

page 11:

$\frac{1}{12}$ acre; 4; $\frac{1}{12}$

page 15:

20 pictures; 20; $\frac{1}{4}$; 5

page 19:

1. 9 times; $3 \div \frac{1}{3} = 9$
2. 6 times; $3 \div \frac{1}{2} = 6$
3. 4 times; $1 \div \frac{1}{4} = 4$

page 20:

$\frac{1}{16}$ ton; 8; $\frac{1}{16}$

page 23:

1. $\frac{1}{8}$ pound; $\frac{1}{2} \div 4 = \frac{1}{8}$
2. $\frac{1}{9}$ pound; $\frac{1}{3} \div 3 = \frac{1}{9}$
3. $\frac{1}{8}$ pound; $\frac{1}{4} \div 2 = \frac{1}{8}$

Problem Solving

1. **a.** 10 times
   b. 6 times
   c. 12 times
   d. 4 times
2. **a.** $\frac{1}{4}$ pizza
   b. $\frac{1}{6}$ pound
   c. $\frac{1}{8}$ quart